House Cleaning Hacks: DIY Cleaning Hacks For A Clean And Organized Home

DIY Reads

TABLE OF CONTENTS

ABOUT DIY READS

At DIY Reads, we aim at offering you high quality, informative and easy to follow DIY guides to help you learn and increase your knowledge and awareness about different subjects.

In today's fast paced world, everyone needs guidance to solve everyday problems with quick, easy and affordable DIY hacks. DIY Reads will help you embark upon your own DIY projects to save you time, money and unnecessary elbow grease.

Our team of high quality and experienced writers and researchers are dedicated to providing you the best content, helping you learn many do-it-yourself projects the easy way!

Introduction

Only a few people consider cleaning their favorite thing in the world. If you can get one of them to come to your home to clean, you're all set to cherish a happy, clean home atmosphere. If not, you are going to have to buckle down and do it yourself.

Fortunately, there are several ways to ensure that you are going to get done faster with far less stress on your back, knees and even your wallet. By following the tips and tricks mentioned in this home cleaning guide, you will not only keep from having to resort to the more dangerous chemicals that assault your nose, but you will also be using things that are better for the environment as well.

Many of the items used in the following tips are probably in your home right now- and most of them will be found in your kitchen cabinets.

The best trick that you can learn is to make things as efficient as possible. Combine chores with one another. Use time saving tricks and shave time off of the jobs that you hate. Find ways to lessen the burden or to make it even a little more pleasant.

Stop making cleaning your home so hard on yourself and you will hate cleaning just a little less.

The Rules of Easy, Effective, Quick And Pain-Free Cleaning

Adopt the Practice of on the Fly Cleaning

Have you ever made a huge meal and then trudged into the kitchen to a sink full of dirty dishes and pans that will need hours of scouring?

Or, have you ever tried on three or four outfits only before coming home to address piles of clothes all over your bedroom floor after an event?

The problem here is that you are saving all of the hard work for last- when you are most likely to be already tired and possibly kind of grumpy.

Instead, do things as you go and you will find that you are spending far less time cleaning up at the end.

In the kitchen: fill a dishpan or sink with hot, soapy water and wash up dishes as you go. Or, you can swish things in the water and then fill the dishwasher as you go. Even if you are going to wash a few things by hand, you can have them soaking and ready to wash while you are eating.

That way, you should only have to give the pans a few swipes with a dishcloth and a good rinse without having to break out the super duty, elbow grease and hours of teeth gritting work.

Keep a cloth nearby to flick over the counters as you go and you won't face grimy cabinets either.

In the bathroom: keep a small rubber squeegee tool in the shower and wipe the walls down before you step out.

Keep a roll of paper towels on the counter for a quick wipe down after you have washed your hands or brushed your teeth.

Mention this trick to others and hope that they follow suit. Use one of the automatic toilet cleaners or get in the habit of throwing in a denture tablet every night so that you rarely have to scrub the toilet at all.

Taming the laundry monster: keep a hamper in the closet and immediately put dirty clothes into it-never on the floor. Have a basket ready for dry cleaning so that you have it all gathered in one place.

Anything that does not fit you or enhance your appearance should be immediately bagged and taken down to donate.

Stop Giving Your Rooms Identity Issues

A bedroom is supposed to be where you sleep. A living room is where you watch television or read or play games with the family. A kitchen or dining room is where you eat. Too many people use these rooms interchangeably and that tends to create more cleaning conundrums.

Most of the surfaces in each of these rooms are perfectly designed for their specific use but not for others. For instance, your bedroom comforter was made to be soft and warm so that it can keep you cozy. It was not meant to repel butter and syrup because you thought breakfast in bed sounded like a great idea.

Unless you like the extra work that these habits create, keep food in the kitchen or dining room, sleep in the bedroom and do living room things in the living room.

Why are You Not Stopping Dirt in the First Place?

The first rule of efficiency is to prevent more work from being created. In the world of cleaning hacks that means that you are going to prevent more dirt from coming in to your home. How do you do this? You start by eliminating the biggest source of dirt there is-shoes.

More dirt comes in on your family's shoes than by any other source. Get them in the habit of taking shoes off at the front or back door and either wearing socks or slippers while inside. If they do this, you will eliminate the dirt that gets shuffled across floors and spread from room to room.

Other things that you can do includes closing windows on high dust days or when there is something that will increase dirt going on. You can also make sure that your furnace vents and ductwork is kept clean, which will also decrease the amount of dust and allergens that will be blown about when the furnace is running.

Replacing filters will do a lot to help in this department but the average duct work is so twisty and long that it should be professionally cleaned at least once every two to three years.

A Little Here, a Little There, Never Finished Anywhere

Have you ever started dusting the living room and then wandered off to wash a few dishes only to get distracted and end up folding towels. Now there are three tasks finished but not a single whole room is clean in the house because you didn't stick with it. It is better to start and finish one room at a time – with a clear goal of what you are doing and not doing.

Do you really need to wash the living room curtains every week? No, you do not.

You don't need to haul out the major cleaning equipment if you keep ahead of the game- so, decide what needs done, schedule out your tasks and then do them and do not leave that room until you are finished. Bring everything you need to that room before you even get started.

That means if you are dusting and vacuuming the living room, grab the vacuum cleaner and your dusting supplies and then hit it.

I Hope I can Do this on Thursday or Something

Hoping for a chance to clean means that you are never going to get a thing done. Set a schedule for yourself and give yourself a reasonable timeframe to work in so that it does not seem overwhelming and then stick to that plan.

The longer you put off your cleaning, the more work will be involved when you finally force yourself to get down to it.

The absolute worst is when you wait until the night before a party or a family visit when you are already stressed out.

Put Some Pep in Your Step and Make Cleaning Fun

Maybe you don't enjoy cleaning but you probably do enjoy listening to your favorite music or maybe watching a favorite movie or television show, so why don't you indulge yourself and get some cleaning done at the same time?

If you would prefer, you can use this time to catch up on some "reading" by loading an audio book on your mp3 player and working while you expand your mind.

Now that you have some helpful tips to get you

motivated and to make the most of your time, let's look at some room by room hacks to make the best use of what you have learned.

In the Kitchen: From Burned Pans to Greasy Counters and More

Using pan liners and non-stick sprays can lessen some of your clean up, but even those will not eliminate 100% of your cleaning issues in the kitchen.

Burned on foods and grease are the two biggest culprits here and will keep you busy if you do not learn some time and work saving tips.

To clean your heavy glass or metal roasting pans

without a lot of effort, you can use the oven or oven cleaner.

Method one: Put the pans into your self-cleaning oven during a cleaning cycle and they should come out perfectly clean. Be careful that you only do this with tempered glass or heavy metal pans because lightweight pans will warp beyond use.

Method two: Spray the pans with an oven cleaner and allow to sit for several hours or even overnight. Be careful though. The fumes of the oven cleaner are very toxic so be sure to have plenty of ventilation and wear gloves to protect your hands when you clean the pans back out.

Disgusting sponges, scrub brushes and other tools can grow mold or bacteria, especially if they are allowed to sit on the counter between uses.

To clean them, throw them into the dishwasher just before you run it- if you run the sterilize cycle, you will kill most of the potentially harmful germs so that you do not spread them around the kitchen.

If you are noticing that your white coffee cups and mugs are stained with coffee or tea or you cannot get your oddly shaped bottles and vases clean, you can throw in a denture cleaning tablet and some warm water. Let the tablet soak and fizz those stains away.

If the vases are really grungy, you can throw in a

small amount of uncooked rice and shake well to loosen any dirt that the denture tabs may not be able to get to.

Copper pots will sparkle and shine with this easy "recipe". Mix flour and salt in a three to one ratio and then add in enough plain white vinegar to make a thick paste. Coat the copper pot with this paste and then let set for about half an hour or so. Rinse well and buff dry.

You can also use non-gel toothpaste to clean copper or silver.

Your coffee carafe will not get stained if you make a habit to rinse it whenever it gets empty and to never let it boil dry. Running a cycle of vinegar through the coffee maker will also keep the whole thing gleaming clean as well.

But, if you do notice that you are starting to get some stains then chill out! Grab some ice cubes and some kosher salt and add to the carafe and then swirl until the stains are gone.

Finish up with a good rinse. Be sure that the carafe is perfectly cool before trying this or you may cause the glass to crack.

Did you know that you are not supposed to wash champagne glasses with soap? The soap will leave a film on the inside of the glass that keeps the bubbles from forming.

Who wants flat champagne?

Hand wash these glasses being careful to keep all soap on the outside only.

Stainless steel appliances look great until they are greasy and marked with fingerprints. Some cleaners will only streak and make a bigger mess and others may dull the appearance of the finish.

A better idea is to use simple white flour on a clean cloth- buff the surface clean and then use a second cloth to wipe away all of the flour.

You know the old saying about fighting fire with fire? Did you know that you can clean oil with oil? It's true and it will keep you from spending hours trying to clean the grease encrusted stove hood or stove top. Using mineral or vegetable oil, dab the surfaces that you are cleaning thoroughly.

This coating of oil will not only break down the bond of the old oil to the surface so that it is far easier to wipe away but will also provide a barrier to any new build up as well.

Gunked up stove burners are usually a nightmare to clean. You can use oven cleaner on them or you can use 1 cup of ammonia and four sealable bags to get them super clean, super easy. Add one quarter cup of the ammonia to each of the bags and then insert the burner.

Seal the bag and leave overnight. Rinse well and you are done. For safety, put the bags in a bucket or the sink in case of a failed seal or a tear.

Make your microwave a self-cleaning appliance by putting one or two cups of water and two tablespoons of white vinegar into a microwaveable bowl. You can add a few drops of essential oil if you would like but this is not necessary.

Microwave the bowl on high for five minutes or so and then wipe the microwave out with a clean cloth.

If you have a lot of burned on pan residue to deal with, there is a simple trick that you should know.

No, you should not throw the pan away when no one is looking!

All that you need to do is scrape out whatever you can being careful not to scrape the bottom of the pan. Next, fill the pan about ¼ of the way up.

Add a few tablespoons of baking soda to the water and then boil for fifteen minutes or so. Most of the gunk should come right out. If the pan is very thickly coated, you may have to repeat this again.

Speaking of baking soda- did you know that you could use it to clean virtually any surface? Baking soda and salt can also be mixed together for even stronger cleaning.

Use a halved lemon (or a lemon rind) and a handful of salt to clean your wooden cutting boards. The lemon will disinfect the boards as well.

Mix one tablespoon of cream of tartar with just a little bit of water and then use the thick paste to clean stainless steel sinks and appliances.

To properly clean and care for your cast iron cookware you should avoid all soap products. Instead pour a few tablespoons of olive oil and some salt into the pan and briskly rub to remove food particles. Rinse and dry carefully and then re-season with fresh oil.

The Bathroom: The Room Where We Get Clean can Get so Dirty!

It is ironic that we go in to shower or bathe our bodies, brush our teeth or wash our hands and end up making this room dirty. Here are some tips to make cleaning it much easier.

After your shower, open the door or curtain all the way to allow the steam to evaporate. Then close the door/curtain once again to allow them to dry but leave a small gap at either end so that air will flow through. This will help to prevent mildew growth and odors.

The next time you are brewing up some tea, pour off a small amount and let it cool completely. Use the cooled tea to wipe down the bathroom mirror and it will gleam.

One of the simplest ways to clean the toilet without harsh chemicals is with vinegar and baking soda. Let this mixture sit for fifteen minutes or so and then flush and all of the stains will be gone.

Use a soft cloth and baby oil to clean your bathroom fixtures and they will sparkle and shine and resist finger prints as well.

Don't leave cans on the sink, floor or bathtub side

because they will leave nasty rust rings that are almost impossible to get rid of. If you can't store these things somewhere else then paint a protective coating of clear nail polish around the bottom to save yourself the trouble.

You can use a halved grapefruit and regular table salt to scrub your tub. You can use any citrus fruit in place of the grapefruit if you would prefer.

Non-stick cooking spray can be used to prevent grime from ever happening in the first place. Be warned thought that this will leave your tub super slippery.

Dryer sheets are perfect for cleaning glass shower doors – the soap scum will come right off.

To prevent a mirror from fogging up you can either rub it with bar soap and the buff clean or do the same thing with creamy style shaving cream.

Here is a simple trick to clean a clogged shower head. Fill a plastic bag with plain vinegar and then wrap it on the shower head.

Tie the bag in place and leave overnight. In the morning pull the bag off and run the shower for a few seconds to rinse. It should be clean and flowing like brand new.

The Bedroom is Your Castle but it Looks Like the Dungeon!

The bedroom is supposed to be your refuge from the world- your inner sanctum and your place of peace. You can't find peace in a room that is in constant disarray or has some strange odor that you can never quite get rid of. Here are some tips to keeping this room more Zen and less animal den.

Everyone loves the look and feel of wall to wall carpeting in the bedroom but it just increases the amount of work that you will do in there. Hardwood is easier to care for and only needs a quick dust mopping once a week.

If you do feel the need to have carpet, choose stain-resistant carpeting.

Once a week wipe down your window sills and other hard wood surfaces with a damp cloth so that you do not get dust build up.

Bedroom curtains should be taken down and washed or changed frequently. If this is not an option then vacuum your curtains often so that dust does not build up in the folds.

Change clothes in the bathroom or keep a hamper in the bedroom so that you never need to leave clothes on the floor.

Make this room a shoe free zone - keep shoes in a hall closet or by the front door if possible.

Air out the bedroom whenever the weather will permit you to do so. A ceiling fan will help to circulate the air as well.

Cover your mattress and the box spring with a dust proof and allergen reducing cover. Choose one that is easy to put on and remove and one that can be easily cleaned if needed.

Avoid all dry clean only bedding, pillows and other materials for your bed. Choose sheets that are easy to care for so that you can wash them frequently.

The tendency to put furniture in the bedroom just adds obstacles to stub your toes on and does nothing to minimize cleaning. The less that you have in there, the less you move around and the less you have to deal with on cleaning day. If you do have furniture in the bedroom beyond the bed, make it easy to care for and non-upholstered.

Since dust mites thrive in warm and humid weather or areas opt for a dehumidifier. Choose one that is big enough for the room.

Make the bedroom a pet free zone. Pets are wonderful parts of the family but they will complicate the cleaning process.

The bedroom should also be a food free zone. The only thing you are doing is making more work for yourself and inviting pests into this room. Eat in the kitchen- you will be glad that you did.

A Liveable Living Room Without the Hours of Cleaning

In many houses the living room is where company comes to visit and the first room that family will see when they come to your home. You want it to look nice but you should not have to spend hours on end to keep it that way.

Grab a basket- whenever you spot something in the living room that does not belong there, chuck it into the basket. Put stuff in the right place at night or once a week.

You can also hold toys or other things hostage until

your children do a chore to earn them back- they will stop leaving stuff in the living room.

Once a week, brush off the couch or flip the cushions. Sweep the crud from under the cushions and pocket the loose change, combs and other oddities that you find. Rearrange the pillows on the couch and go on with the rest of the cleaning.

Wipe down the coffee table and other hard surfaces. You don't really need to use furniture polish but if you want to, then go lightly with the spray.

Vacuum the floor- sprinkle some baking soda or baking soda mixed with cinnamon on the floor for a fresh scent as you go.

If you notice scratches or other marks on your wood surfaces you can repair them with markers or crayons. If the marks are deep you may have to build the surface up a bit so that it is even.

Use socks, water and vinegar to clean your blinds and you will cut the task's time in half. Mix up warm water and a few tablespoons of vinegar. Put socks on both hands. Wet one hand with the water and vinegar and then wipe the blinds down. Dry with the other sock covered hand.

Greener Cleaners: Save Money and the Environment with these Homemade Cleaners

Baking soda can be used on virtually every surface to clean, deodorize and scour. You can also use it in your laundry and to open clogged drains. It makes sense to stock up on lots of baking soda because you will use it so often.

Borax is also great for laundry, cleans, deodorizes and disinfects. It can also be used to repel pests like roaches.

White vinegar will cut through grease and soap scum can be used to inhibit mold and can also be used to clear clogged drains.

Kosher salt can be used to scour with and will also disinfect.

For the following recipes you will need either a jar or a spray bottle.

A tub and tile cleaner: 1 2/3 cups of baking soda, ½ cup of liquid vegetable soap or castile soap, ½ cup of water and two tablespoons of vinegar. Shake this up to mix. Clean your desired surface and then rinse well.

A better scouring powder: All that you will need is a cup each of baking soda, borax and salt. Sprinkle on whatever surface you are cleaning, wipe down , rinse and then buff dry.

Toilet cleaner without the harsh chemicals: ¼ cup of borax or baking soda if you prefer. One cup of vinegar. Let soak for 15 minutes, swish with a toilet brush if needed and then flush.

A better glass cleaner: ¼ cup of vinegar plus four cups of warm water in a spray bottle. Use a soft cloth or old newspaper to wipe off.

Drain cleaner and clog buster: ½ cup of baking soda and 1 cup of vinegar. Pour in the baking soda first and then the vinegar. This will fizz up rather dramatically. Put the drain on once the fizzing slows down and leave alone for 15 minutes.

Pour plenty of hot water down the drain and the clog should be gone. If not, you can repeat this process until the clog is busted and the drain is flowing freely. Use this recipe once a week to prevent clogs from forming in the future.

Sanitize your kitchen and bathroom floors with ½ cup of borax mixed in two gallons of hot water. You do not have to rinse after this.

If you have calcium or lime deposits you can soak a towel in plain vinegar and then wrap it around the faucets overnight.

To get rid of mold or mildew mix borax and vinegar (1/2 cup of each) to form a paste and then brush or sponge on to the affected areas. You can leave this mixture sit for several hours and then rinse off.

A better tub scrubber: 1 cup of baking soda plus ½ cup of castile or vegetable oil soap. If you would like, you can add several drops of your favorite essential oils to this mixture.

An all-purpose cleaner perfect for

every room of your house: 1 teaspoon baking soda, 1 or 2 teaspoons of dish soap, 2 tablespoons of plain vinegar. Put all ingredients into a spray bottle and then add enough water to fill. If you would like, you can add essential oils to this mixture as well.

Save citrus rinds to grind in the garbage disposal last so that it has a nice aroma when all is said and one.

Wood polish: mix the juice of half a lemon and a tablespoon each of olive oil and water. Use a soft cloth to buff your furniture. Discard any leftovers.

Homemade Stain Removers

Stains do not need to be the end of the world. Some stains may seem hopeless but here are a few tips for some of the most common ones.

Red wine spills - blot as much of the liquid as possible. (Grab a white towel or you may risk adding insult to injury by transferring dyes to the stain as you work). Once you have dabbed away as much of the liquid as possible you can use hydrogen peroxide to remove most of the dye.

Be warned: this will also remove the dye from the carpet or fabric that you are applying it to. You can also try using adding dish soap to the peroxide to blot at the stain. (This will also work for most types of ink stains as well.)

For coffee stains - mix an egg yolk with warm water and then dab on.

For other stains, whip ½ cup of dish detergent with ½ cup of warm water with your mixer or your blender and then apply to the stain. Shampoo will also work in place of the dish detergent.

Make Your Own Laundry Detergent

You will need a bar of laundry soap (look for these in the laundry aisle at most grocery stores. Name brands include Fels Naptha and Ivory). You will also need a box of borax, 1 box of baking soda, essential oils if you would like to add scent to your detergent.

First, grate the bar of laundry soap and then mix with the other ingredients. You can store this in a sealed bucket or a large jar. To use add 1 tablespoon of your prepared mixture for a regular or lightly soiled load of clothes and 2 tablespoons for heavier soil or a larger load.

You can also make your own fabric softener to go with your homemade laundry soap. You will just add ½ cup of baking soda to the washer before you add the clothes or you can add ¾ cup to one cup of pure vinegar to the wash or rinse cycle.

The ultimate: mix ½ cup of pure vinegar, ½ cup of baking soda and just ½ the amount of your favorite detergent to get clean, soft and static clean free clothes.

To freshen clothes between washings – mix 2 tablespoons of vinegar, 2 tablespoons of liquid fabric softener and several drops of an essential oil of your choice (you can use almond or vanilla extract if you would prefer)

Pour this into a spray bottle and then fill with water. Shake up the contents and spritz on the clothing.

Conclusion

THANK YOU for downloading this book. Hopefully, this book has helped you in learning a few more tips, tricks and hacks to hone your home cleaning skills.

Printed in Great Britain
by Amazon

34550375R00036